Dedicated to my parents and all my teachers
who taught that I can achieve anything when
I work hard, smart and pay attention.

-Krishna K.Virwani

Thank you Dadu, Dadi, Tatha and Patti for teaching me good moral values. I love you Mommy and Dada. Thank you for all the love you shower and the sacrifices you have made for me. You are the best parents in the whole universe.

My sincere thanks to my teachers - Mrs. Stearns, Mrs. Cuttrel, Mrs. Von Motts, Mrs. Khosravi, Ms. Avalos, and Mrs. Verma for giving me the best education. I learned a lot from you.

Special thanks to Mrs. Khanna and my awesome illustrator for making my dream come true.

Thank you Guruji and Bhagvati ji for your blessings and grace. I love you infinitely.

- Krishna K. Virwani

My First Book of Poems- by Krishna K. Virwani

First Edition April 2022
Poems authored by Krishna K. Virwani
Illustrations by Mannat Tyagi
ISBN ---- 978-0-578-28585-6
Published by Amazon KDPc

My First Book of Poems

By Krishna K. Virwani

Acrostic Poems

Acrostic Poem

A word is the topic

Capitalize each first letter

Rhyming is unnecessary

One letter starts each line

Short phrases describe the word

Terse

Interesting, fun and

Creative in every way!

The Star of Winter

Silently from the sky.

Now it is falling.

Oh! what a lovely sight!

Welcome to winter's white fun!

Happy Birthday O' King!

Cute little baby is born.

Happy in a simple barn.

Rose the star of Bethlehem,

In Mary and Joseph's hands.

Smiling like a billion suns!

The Magi gave presents.

Messenger of God is HE.

Angels, animals and Shepherds say-

"Savior! Wish you a Happy Birthday!"

Favourite Person of Mine

Fabulous and full of fun.

Always cares about me.

Teaches me patiently,

Hero !

Encouraging and Loving ever,

Really the world's best "Dada" !

#1

I   DAD   U

Shape
Or
Concrete
Poems

A Concrete poem is a poem that is shaped like the thing it describes. The shape adds to the meaning of the poem, like this one.

SMILE

Krishna's Frosty Friend

Guess who I am? I was a winter guest at Krishna's home in Boise. He built me with snow from tummy to teeth. He gave me a scarf and hat, just like his own! My warm black coat was shiny with sparkly stones. With carrot nose and pebbly smile, I was a handsome man!

Teachers - The light of the World

Thank you my teachers
For everything you do

Sunshine
Brightens the world

Teachers
Enlighten our minds

Thank you teachers
for the light of knowledge that will shine in me forever and ever.

Thank you
Sunshine
For the sunny sky, blue

Sunshine
Helps plants make food

O Teachers !
I shine because of you!

Sunshine
Reveals the world to you

Teachers
Help to think things through

Reduce! Reuse! Recycle! Stop polluting patient Earth! Ouch! No more wars! Achoo! Smoky cars! Yikes! Smelly litter everywhere! Oh! Please do take care.

Loving Mother Earth

An Amazing Mollusc!

Meet my dear friend, the smart octopus!

Nine brains - one in the head and one in each arm.

Eight nifty tentacles, swishing along.

Suckers touch and taste its prey.

Camouflage is its forte!

It zips like a jet and escapes.

Oh! Beware of its inky spray.

Three healthy hearts to pump its blood blue.

Ha! Ha! Not one funny bone to tickle through.

Ha! Ha!

Haiku Poems

Haiku

Poem in three lines,
With seventeen syllables.
Five, seven, five rule.

Winter Slumber

Snowy white blanket
Covers my furry friend's den
Sweet dreams, Baby fox!

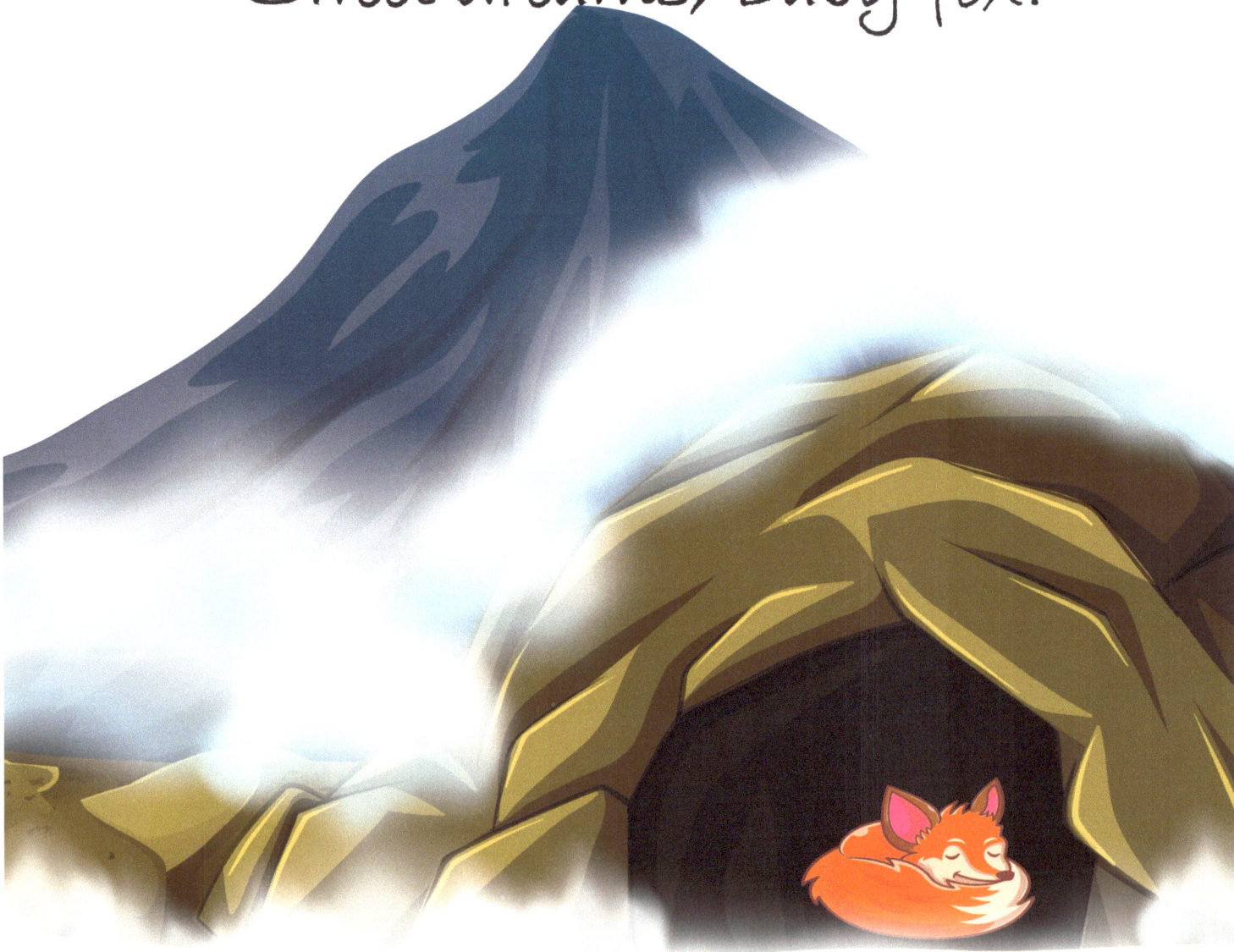

Mothers - Our Protectors!

CLUCK! CLUCK! Squeaked the bush!
An angry mother flew out.
Cheep! Cheep! Baby Chicks!

Online Student

Long videos I see.
Studying hard day and night.
Success! Here I come!

CHANGE

A caterpillar,
Transforms into butterfly.
Change! Constant in life!

Limerick
Poems

Limerick
A short poem of five lines!
"A,A,B,B,A" pattern of rhyme.
Funny and silly,
It tickles your belly,
Five syllables for "B", "A" has nine!

 Slip!  Drip!  Wisp!

He is Ice - the Winter King!
Freezes the planet, until spring!
He is strong and stout.
Oh! The Sun is out...
He is *melting, melting* now *missing!*

The Rainbows!

When the sunlight hits the raindrop right,
It splits into seven colors bright!
The green clovers gleam!
A leprechaun's dream!
Trick, ya! No gold do rainbows hide!

The Princess' groom!

The beautiful fair princess of Rhode,
Married a handsome prince, brave and bold!
She ran to her love true,
Tripped on a stinky shoe,
And kissed a slimy toad on the road!

Jelly Tummy!

When I came from school, 'twas funny!
I had a groaning growling tummy.
I looked around for food,
The green jelly looked good.
Jelly in my hungry belly. Yummy! Yummy!

www.ingramcontent.com/pod-product-compliance
Lightning Source LLC
LaVergne TN
LVHW072102070426
835508LV00002B/226